CHANGE YOUR BEHAVIOR, CHANGE YOUR RESULTS

A Women's Journey

by

MARIAH D'LAINE WACHA, B.A.
Certified Professional Life Coach
Clinical Hypnotherapist

www.TotalPublishingAndMedia.com

ISBN: 978-1-937829-02-5

Why read this book

Dear Friends,

I am on a journey. If you are reading this book, more than likely you are on a similar journey. Through trials, tribulations, and a few errors, I have learned a few things about life I feel are invaluable. This book is for all of the women who don't understand why they keep making the same mistakes over and over. I know what it is like to be lied to, cheated on and stabbed in the back. I have been through many relationships in my life, some great and some really awful. I have to admit that I am not proud of some of my behavior in my past, but I also feel I have to tell the truth. I have not been perfect in my life, but I have worked very hard over many years to understand why I did what I did. This book will help you to understand and analyze the self-sabotage and self-destructive behavior we sometimes engage in.

It will cover how we are programmed from birth to act and behave in certain ways that are not always flattering. This book is intended for the sole purpose of helping women to gain their power back and achieve a new understanding of their magnificence. I want women to regain their self-esteem and self-worth so that we can raise a new generation of strong, powerful, confident young women. It's time to be fierce and take charge of your life. You are worth the time and energy to live your life to the fullest.

I hope that when you read this, at least one of the life lessons I have learned will ring true to you. I want to help you continue your journey with a little more knowledge and a little less pain. I believe it is our duty, as women, to pass on good advice whenever possible to further aid in gaining back our voice and self-worth as women. Even though much of the examples used throughout this book are my own, the lessons and epiphanies are from interviews with many of my girlfriends and the men in my life.

If we are ever going to change the world, we have to begin with ourselves. I do think women really rule the world; we have just let men think they do. You have a lot more influence than you have been led to believe. If you are ready to take responsibility for you actions and change your life, then let's get busy and pass it on.

God Bless all women, and good luck on your journey.

Acknowledgements

I want to give my enormous gratitude to all of my family and friends for all of their continued love and support. I would not have done this without them. I also want to thank all of the people I have encountered over the years who have given me a wealth of material. I have learned a lot from them. To my amazing son who makes me want to be a better person and mother. He is everything to me.

Most of all, thank you to the love of my life, Mike. What would I ever do without your endless love and patience? I haven't always been the easiest person to live with these past twenty years. I love and adore you and appreciate you more than words can ever say.

To all women throughout history who have risked everything, pushed the boundaries, refused to take no for an answer, but also stood up for their beliefs and said "NO MORE". Thank you from the bottom of my heart.

"Well-behaved women rarely make history."

Laurel Thatcher Ulrich

Table of Contents

She Who Cares the Least Wins!

L et me explain what I mean when I say, "She Who Cares the Least Wins." We, as women, care so much about other people, and what they think, that we sometimes forget to take care of ourselves and what we think. Women tend to make sure everyone else has what they need and then take whatever love or attention is left over for themselves. The neglect we heap on ourselves diminishes our true brilliant authentic selves. No one gets to appreciate our magnificence because we never show it. Most of us feel unworthy of praise and love and can rarely take any compliments. We are taught that it is conceited to think we are amazing and that self-loathing and constant criticism of ourselves are acceptable behavior. We are told to take care of others and not be too much the center of attention. I believe we need to start caring more about nurturing ourselves so we can then truly be magnificent for all of our loved ones. Care less about what others think and you will win more of your true self back. What you think and believe about yourself matters. In fact, it's all that matters. I want to tell you the story of how I discovered this Mantra of "She Who Cares the Least Wins".

It all came about one evening about a year ago when one of my dearest friends came over to visit for the evening. We sat in my cozy living room drinking wine and trying to solve the mysteries of relationship problems between men and women. No small feat I'm telling you. Men and women have been confused by each other's behavior since birth. However, this night I really had some interesting insights. Let me give you a little background to set the stage. My friend got married when she was very young, right out of high school, and had one son. Now she was divorced and had been back in the dating world for about ten years. I, on the other hand, had dated extensively when I was young and had completely given up on men when I suddenly met and married the man of my dreams. I had chased the dream of happily ever after until I was exhausted. When I finally gave up and decided that all men were lying, cheating jerks, and I was going to pursue my career, my wonderful husband appeared. Everyone kept telling me to quit looking and just date and have fun, but I didn't know how. I would start dating someone and immediately try his last name on to see if it fit. Boy, have I learned a lot since then, which is another reason I am writing this book. Anyway, I am still very happily married after twenty years. She and I both agreed that good men can be hard to find and I know deeply how lucky I am. My husband is a wonderful man and my best friend. He understands women and has this great ability to help my girlfriends understand a man's behavior. They all come to him and ask, "Why is he doing this?" or, "What did he mean when he said that?"

My friends and I wish we could just clone him or do seminars on understanding men. My girlfriend and I told him that he should start a training school for men, but he just laughed and said, "The problem is that, the men who really need it wouldn't come because they don't know they need it." We realized that he was absolutely right and all of us burst out laughing!

My husband gets it. He is the first to point out, however, that he hasn't always been this way. He also had some growing up to do. Bless his heart, he's really modest about how great he is. I also have to give a lot of credit to my mother-in-law. She talked to him a lot when he was growing up about how to treat women like ladies. She also told him not to put up with being treated badly either. He doesn't take crap from anybody, I promise you. Thank God he listened! Great job, mom! It wasn't until many years later that I came to understand that we, as humans, create our own reality. We bring things, people, and events into our lives unknowingly most of the time through the "Law of Attraction". It is a fact that what you think about and focus on, you *will* bring about! However, I will get into that later in the book. Now, let me get back to the story.

My friend and I were in a deep discussion that evening and the conversation went something like this:

My friend: I really don't understand it. It seems that when I treat a guy badly, I can't get rid of him; and when I am completely there for him and dote on him, he ignores me and treats me badly." I'm being polite by the way when I say 'badly'.

Me: I remember that always happening to me too! I would treat them like a king, and they would leave me and go back to the crazy ex-girlfriend who they supposedly hated because they screamed at them all of the time. They would tell me how much they hated her and then leave me to go back to her. REALLY? Are you kidding me? I would be left feeling dumbfounded.

As the conversation progressed we decided that from now on, if she was ever going to have any sense of balance in the relationship, she would have to change her "Mode of Operation". We felt she would have to learn to care more about herself and her needs and less about them if she was going to keep from getting her heart broken. Suddenly, I remembered a phrase that my husband would often use when joking around about relationships: "He who cares the least wins." He had heard it on the "Lex and Terry" show on talk radio. I thought it was very appropriate. So, that night my friend and I adopted it and from then on it became the mantra by which all relationships would proceed. So thank you, Lex and Terry!

From that night on, when she would get overly involved with a new man and her own identity would begin to disappear, I would be obligated, as the good friend that I proclaimed to be, to remind her: "She who cares the least wins." To our absolute shock, it worked!

It even worked if there was another woman involved. If there was a rival, she would simply tell him, "Hey, whatever. I don't have time to play games. If you decide you want to go out with me and I am still available we'll talk." The reaction would be almost instant. Creating this sense of urgency was brilliant. Being indifferent and almost dismissive was like an aphrodisiac. She would become more attractive because she was appearing to be unavailable, which made him want her even more. Men are hunters and love the hunt, so let them! Now, this didn't mean she wasn't nervous and feeling completely insecure when she acted in this manner. However, she discovered the price of losing her dignity became too high when it came to groveling to keep him around. I've heard of this concept in sales but never in relationships. Normally, I hate "Game Playing" but self preservation is critical for your own self esteem.

The guy would be blown away because she wasn't turning into a whining insecure woman who was begging for his presence and attention. Over time, it really became a private joke between us, but I began to wonder on a deeper level why this approach worked. Why would a man seem to prefer being treated terribly and want to stay as opposed to being doted on? That's where this little endeavor began. I began to seriously ask myself as well as all of my friend's questions about their past relationships. What a wealth of information they shared. We all agreed that we should impart the few tidbits of knowledge that we had learned over the years. Hopefully, it would help prevent other women from experiencing some of the pain in their relationships. At least that is our hope. We have since changed the Mantra a little and learned a lot more, but the meaning behind it is still valid. You have to put yourself first. It's not selfish to care about the most important person in your life: *You*. Now, we encourage each other to care differently, not less.

I purposely kept this book as short and sweet and to the point as possible because I believe women have enough to take care of on any given day and you either get it or you don't. I believe you'll get it. So from my friends and me to you and yours I truly wish you all the best in all your relationships. Something else very interesting happened to me through this endeavor. I have discovered that I am a much happier wife, mother, and friend if I make sure and take some time for myself. If I don't take that time for myself, I find my stress level rises and I get more irritable and downright bitchy! I feel stretched too thin. I used to think that if I didn't spend every waking moment in service of others, I wasn't a good representation of womanhood. I would worry what other people would think and say about me too. I imagined them looking at me and saying, "Can you believe her? Who does she think she is, taking care of herself instead of her family? That is so selfish of her!" Well, guess what? No one cares what I do. It's just like Dr. Phil says, "You wouldn't worry about what people thought about you if you knew how little they did." Or something to that affect. Anyway, my point is that I don't spend my days thinking about what my friends are doing. I'm too busy with my own life and they are, too; so get over it. I made a decision that every time I slip back into that frame of mind, I make myself stop it and move on. If someone in your life is verbally judging you I can guarantee that it's their own insecurities that they are projecting onto you, so you must realize that and let it go. Most of the time, they just don't want you to be better because then you will move on and won't be their friend anymore. They want you to stay put right where you are, in negative patterns. Don't listen! Please continue on your own path and wish them well on their journey. This is one instance when you can say, "It's you, not me." I have to move on. You just have to laugh at the moment and get busy living your own dreams and somehow life will unfold before you as it was meant to, and you will rise.

It Begins

Ok, lets' get started. This is my theory of the evolution of women, and all humor is completely intended and, unfortunately, I think dead on. Here is some food for thought at least. When we are born, our parents looked at us and said, "It's a beautiful baby girl"! Without intending to, they automatically put into affect a set of guidelines that you would be programmed with from birth. You will play house with your dolls, wear dresses and makeup, spend countless hours worrying about your hair, clothes, etc.

If you had been born a boy it would have been cars, trains, dinosaurs, jeans, and any given uniform (football, baseball, etc.). So I believe this is where the mindset begins. We learn our roles at an early age and most of us know how to play them very well. The few that try to break out of the mold and buck the system are quickly reprimanded and made to feel horrible until they conform. I think this is the leading cause of teenage suicide. The lack of tolerance for other people's individuality is a worldwide epidemic. Human beings can be so awful to each other. Don't get me started on some of the horrible things I have heard about man's inhumanity to man. There are many examples of atrocities worldwide. So, for now, let's get back to my theory of progression of the life of women.

By the time we progress to school age, the years of programming has become ingrained. Once again there are distinct differences defined between males and females. For instance, there have been many studies proving that boys are given more of the teachers' time and attention than the girls. Everyone assumes that boys are better in math and science classes, although I have seen quite the opposite can be true. Studies have also been conducted to find out if your name can affect how a person pre-judges you. They did an amazing experiment where they used essays as a measuring tool to discover how people feel without ever having met you. The essays were all written very well and all should have all received high scores. The only differences were the names on the top of the paper. At first, they used popular names like Stephanie, Jennifer, Britney, etc. What I refer to as "girly-girl names" and I don't mean that in a bad way; it's just my observation and opinion. They had male names too but you get the point. The essays all received high grades. Then they took the same exact essays and changed the names to ones that were considered less attractive names like Hazel, Harriet, and Gertrude, etc. I'm sure you can guess what the results were. That's right! They all received significantly lower grades even though the term papers were exactly the same.

So, my point is that from the time we are born, there are certain subconscious and cultural differences that can begin to sabotage our self-esteem as women. We begin judging our environment from a very young age. There are a million others factors and criteria that I believe directly affect a woman's' self-esteem such as: too tall; too short; any physical attribute; perceived facial attractiveness; ethnic background; economic background. . . . I could go on but you get the idea. Oh, and let us not forget, the *biggest* issue for women I believe is, how much you weigh! However, we don't have all day and I'm sure you get my point anyway, right? We have to stop constantly comparing ourselves to others instead of appreciating the things we do like about ourselves. Beating yourself up about what you have or don't have is a complete waste of time. Unless you are willing to go under the knife, you are who you are. There is only one"YOU" so you might as well be brilliant at being you! So, let's move on.

Now that we have all of this GARBAGE (and I do mean GARBAGE) programmed in our heads to deal with, let's bring on puberty. Yippee! What kind of fresh hell is this? It's bad enough that we now have the "monthly" issue to deal with and hormones that are raging inside; but let's pile on more to deal with shall we??? Puberty is where only the strong survive and the weak are cut from the herd with vicious scrutiny. Here are just some of the few criteria to measure up. You had better wear the right clothes, shoes, accessories, and so on. Make-up and hair must be done to perfection. All thoughts will begin to center around the most important thing: boys. If you do not have a very strong sense of self-worth established by this time you are in really big trouble.

Our opinion of ourselves and our worthiness can get shoved to the back of the bus behind our peers and men. We also begin to allow them to tell us whether or not we are worthy of associating with at any given time. I wish to God that someone would have told me to get a hobby! Find out what you like to do and do it no matter what anyone says. Trust me, you will have a lot more fun and less pain if you find your own interests that fulfill you. Quit focusing all of your self-esteem and self-worth on your peers and the opposite sex, because you will never be good enough when you're being judged!

Boy! That information would have saved me and a lot of others a huge amount of heartache, But NOOOOO. I was consumed like most other young girls with whether or not this boy or that boy liked me or my best friend more. My favorite childhood movie, by the way was *Cinderella*. Yikes, that says a lot about me, doesn't it? Of course, I pretended I was Cinderella and had to put up with the evil stepsisters until my prince came to rescue me. I now realize I should have been saving myself.

This movie brings up another huge issue that I want to address, which is jealousy between women. This is a huge pet peeve of mine. I don't believe there is anything worse or less attractive than a catty, backstabbing, conniving female. This kind of female is the most insecure and the most vicious of the bunch and unfortunately known to all of us! BEWARE! Avoid them if you can because they are nothing but trouble. I have really never understood why some women are so mean. As women, we have so much to navigate in life without treating each other with contempt, suspicion and sometimes downright loathing. By the way, I just want to insert that I really do have two stepsisters but I love them dearly and we have always gotten along wonderfully. Just thought I had better put that in there! Love you Tonya and Teresa.

Anyway, back to women and their jealousy. I have thought a lot about this and this is my theory: I believe it all stems from what I call the "Pack Mentality". Just go with me on this for a minute. I want you to imagine a herd of animals in the wild as an example. This "herd" would be the same as your circle of friends, family, work, colleagues, etc. Your little universe that you live in would be your "herd".

In the wild, there are only so many males and females who are considered to be attractive by the pack. The leaders have to be the strongest, smartest, and so on to make sure the pack survives. Therefore, they are also, obviously, the most desirable for a mate. It's really the same for human beings, but with much more dire consequences than just survival because we add emotions to the mix. Now, let's look at this from the outside of the picture. I hope right now you're imagining something you have seen on the Discovery channel. I want you to observe the "herd" in your mind. Picture them roaming some grassy field somewhere in Montana. Okay, for a female, of the species, to be considered mating material by the best males, she must achieve certain qualities. First, she must make herself more attractive than any of the rest of the females in order to get his attention. Next, she must successfully sabotage any and all rival females to get the "Good Ones". She must strut her stuff shamelessly until she finally gets her man. So, yeah she has achieved her goal and won her dream guy, right? In the wild everything is fabulous and everyone is happy. Woo-hoo!

However, what happens in human relationships is a very predictable and unfortunate outcome. It happens something like this from my experience: The first thing women do is congratulate themselves on having successfully killed off all rival females to obtain this "prize male". Next, they soon discover that he is completely different than what he represented himself to be and now, they don't want him anymore. They now see that he is a completely gorgeous, attractive jerk. To make matters worse, after he gets to be intimate with you, he is off to be with all of the other females he can conquer. Now, they are left feeling stupid and naive. Of course in the wild the females of the herd could care less because they don't have the complex emotions to deal with like human beings. They are only keeping the herd thriving. I sometimes envy them because it's such a simple way of life. For women, however, it can be devastating because a lot of the time they have ruined friendships and have hurt other women deliberately for a guy they no longer want. Crazy isn't it?

I wish I could say that this trend ends as we mature. However, I still see way too many women consumed with what men think of them instead of finding their own value. They not only criticize themselves but other women, and are usually miserable in their life and don't understand why.

By the time we have reached our twenties, we have been completely brainwashed by television, magazines, friends, parents, YouTube, etc., and one of my favorite past times, the movies. Movies are, in my opinion the worst culprit because, the women in movies set a standard of beauty that would take an army of people for a regular women to achieve. We get into a kind of cattle mentality of being accepted and fitting in the "it" crowd. We have no idea who we are, much less what we want out of life. We develop no identity that is our own, and a personality that reflects what the" media" says is acceptable behavior for women. I fell into this trap also because I didn't even know what questions to ask or actions to take to take charge of my life. I, like most of my friends, continued to look outside of myself and let others tell me whether I was acceptable or not. Heaven forbid I wouldn't be in the "it" crowd. I thought I would literally die if I wasn't accepted. Even then, I felt like there's was something fundamentally wrong with wanting to belong so badly. However, at the same time, I felt powerless to stop myself from trying every new thing on the market to further perfect myself and fit in the "it" crowd.

In our teens and twenties, we live in a tiny little click of the real world and everything that happens to us does feel like life and death. Therefore, we are, of course, drama queens. I remember feeling that if my hair wasn't perfect I couldn't possibly leave the house! What would people think of me? Now, I'm in my forties and very happily married, and life doesn't feel uncertain anymore. I weep for the woman I was then, and at the same time realize that it was necessary in order to evolve. I recall an Oprah show one day where she was talking about a break up she had experienced in her twenties. She said that she was devastated and felt like hanging on to his bumper as he was driving away saying, "Don't go! Please, I love you. No one will ever love you like I do!" or some such nonsense that we woman say. I really can relate to that experience, which I'm sure you can too. I have broken hearts and had my heart broken. I dated into the triple digits, before I found a few of the secrets to retaining some integrity in oneself. That's just one of reasons this book came to be. I hope that by writing this book and confiding a lot of my pitfalls and self analysis I will help one woman go through a little less pain. If I can impart just a few things that I have learned along my journey and it helps, then I will consider one of my life's goals met.

It's very difficult to begin to work on your inside when everything we see tells us it's what's on the outside that matters. I believe that's the true irony of life. We are trained to believe that what's on the outside is what matters, but in order to really be free, you have to adjust your thinking and realize it's what's on the inside that counts. We are finally, in this century, beginning to address this issue. In a perfect world, we would be judged by what we contribute to society with our minds and deeds, not our bodies; but it's far from a perfect world. It's up to each of us to help each other in any way we can to get back our confidence and value ourselves for the glorious creatures that the universe created.

Also, I want to let you know, I am far from perfect in this particular category. I am always learning and consider myself a student of life. I still fall victim to the "I have to look like this or that to be accepted" mentality. I am human after all. It's awful, but as I said, I am continuing to grow and learn and I am very proud of how far I have come thus far. God knows I keep on trying. We all have issues that we wish were different. I want you to start trying to love yourself a little more everyday and realize you are amazing just the way God made you. TAKE BACK YOUR POWER AND VOICE WHAT YOU WANT!! YOU DESERVE TO BE HAPPY!! Amen, Sista!

The Black Hole Syndrome

O ne of the most painful and lonely times in my life was when I was in college. Ironically, however, it actually turned out to be the time I grew the most spiritually. Sometimes, we don't understand why things happen until we get on the other side of a situation. Then, of course, we have twenty-twenty vision. I know now that everything that has ever happened to me lead me to the person I am today. Each experience both good and bad was for a reason. I try not to live with any regrets because it's a waste of time and spirit. In college, however, I felt much differently. I felt like life happened to me and I had no control. My mother and stepfather were living overseas; my siblings lived in other cities so we weren't able to get together very often. I literally had no family support and didn't know anyone in town except a distant relative I really didn't know.

It was the first time I was alone in a new town, starting my third year in college in an apartment all by myself. I remember the silence of that apartment at times would feel deafening. It was decorated beautifully, thanks to my parent's assistance, and was right across the street from the college. I felt like the bird in the gilded cage. I was extremely lonely, but I was too shy to get out and meet people. If I had been all enlightened and self confident, I would have looked at this as an amazing opportunity for an adventure. It could have been a wonderful time to meet new people and experience new things. That is not what happened, however, as I said before, I was a work in progress. I was extremely shy and insecure about everything about myself. Even though I was considered to be attractive, I would constantly criticize myself mentally. The little voice in my mind could be very vicious. I really had no idea who I was, or what I wanted, much less what I wanted to be when I grew up. I felt extremely lost. I was the youngest child of four and had always been the follower. I felt like I was always running trying to catch up. I had always turned to others to tell me what to do and how to get by in life, but now they were all gone and I was alone. I knew who I should pretend to be and how I was supposed to act, etc., but Inside I was a mess. I'm telling you this because I believe all women (and men) have felt this insecurity at some time in their life and I really want you to understand that if you're there now, you are not alone. I know what you are feeling because I was there and I'm telling you it does get better; so hang in there and keep reading!

The good part about this time in my life was that I had no options of running away or changing my situation. I was forced to find a way to deal with my new life and situation. That trapped feeling was awful, but it turned out to be incredibly useful in the end. Of course you would have never convinced me back then that things would work out just fine. When you are alone with just your thoughts one of two things happen. You either learn to feel good or learn to feel bad. It's really that simple and it's always your choice.

My first days were spent watching T.V., going to the grocery store, checking the mail box, reading books and magazines. That was all I did until my first semester in college started. I was too chicken to venture far from my apartment for fear of getting lost. This was way before G.P.S. When I look back now, I think how sad it was that I was so afraid. As you can see, I was the extreme opposite of adventurous. I was so scared of everything. I also realized that I had no idea how to entertain myself because I had no interests or hobbies of my own. My life had been consumed with trying to fit in to this group or that one. I listened to what everyone else thought I should do instead of trusting the voice in my heart. When school did finally start, I began to make some friends and meet a handful of people that expanded my limited world. Once, I had finally established a routine, I settled into college very easily, because I knew what was expected of me. In that sense, I was like a trained monkey that knew how to perform its trained tricks. Go to class, smile at the teacher, be polite, turn in all assignments on time, study hard for all tests, etc, etc, etc. Above all else, I had to be the "Good Little Girl" I had always been expected to be. I never wanted to disappoint anyone especially my family. Does any of this sound familiar? It was definitely my comfort zone.

That area of my life I understood, and I could easily control the outcome by just doing the required work. However, on the inside I was a bundle of insecurities and self doubt. I was convinced that everyone else around me had their lives together and could handle anything that life threw at them. I often wondered what was wrong with me. Why did I always feel so scared inside? Did anyone else feel this way? If they did I never knew it. To me everyone else seemed completely confident in themselves and their abilities. What is hilarious to think about now is they probably looked at me and thought I was the confident one. I can't help but laugh because now when I ask people about that time in their life they all confess to being a mental mess. How crazy life can be sometimes, but we are not alone in the human experience.

I felt like I was this huge empty vessel looking for anything to fill me up and make me whole. Unfortunately, it usually came in the form of a man. Any time I would meet someone new, I would latch on to him like gorilla glue. He became the complete distraction, so I didn't feel that lonely feeling. Plus I didn't have to deal with my issues. I would completely consumed by his world and all the while thinking this is what I was supposed to do and be. I had grown up with T.V. shows like "Brady Bunch," "Hazel,, "Bewitched," "I Dream of Jeanie," etc. The women they depicted were ALWAYS doting on someone. They were loving, supportive and, of course, perfect at nurturing everyone around them. We never heard about their dreams, aspirations, or careers. I had all of these images from the movies, T.V., and magazines of how to be in a relationship. From this point it would take anywhere from one week to three months for the guy to leave skid marks at my door. I couldn't figure out what I was doing wrong. After all, I did everything I had watched on T.V. or read about in those books and magazines. You know the ones I'm talking about right ladies? The ones that tell us all about "how to please your man." What a load of crap. I would cook dinner for them, do their laundry and any other tasks they wanted including sex of course. I was a hugely deluded woman. I really believed that if I did all of those things including sleep with him, then he would love me. Never realizing, I was only a conquest. After all, that's what he told me in the beginning of our relationship. "Of course I'll still want you and want to be with you afterwards." Sound familiar ladies? Don't even get me started on all of the other lies I've heard and then later found out it was just another bullshit line. Pardon my French. Men really do have a bunch of lines they feed women. I was very gullible and extremely naive back in those days.

Anyway, that's not what I want to talk about at this juncture. What I couldn't see was that I was creating this self sabotaging behavior because I had no identity of my own. I was a black hole of constant fear, insecurities and serious need with no clue how to fix myself. I kept looking outside of myself to men, and friends for acceptance. I needed to hear constantly that he loved me, needed me and would never leave me. Was I pretty enough, thin enough, smart enough, etc? How exhausting that must have been. When you constantly have to reassure your partner of their worthiness to be in the relationship, you will never succeed. No one can fill that kind of need from someone else. What's really sad is the only time I didn't act like a black hole of need is when a man who was also a "Black Hole of Need" would latch on to me. This poor guy would be as needy and pathetic as I had been so, naturally I would drop him like a hot potato for being a pathetic insecure wreck. I find the irony in life amazing.

The entire time, I couldn't see that I was a mirror image of him. Then to add insult to injury I would find out that after my desired man had left me, he would have gone back to the ex-girlfriend that he had told me he couldn't stand because she nagged him all the time. That would really hurt, and this scenario seemed to happen to me over and over. I would throw myself a huge pity party of "why didn't he love me? What's wrong with me?'' I did everything for him! I was always there for him. Yada, Yada, Yada, as Seinfeld would say. Wah, Wah, Wah. It was really so sad because I didn't know how to change the behavior to get different results. So, the insanity would continue.

What I know now is that what he liked about her was the appearance of self-confidence. Whether or not she really had confidence didn't matter. She wasn't a black hole of need that was draining him like an emotional vampire. What's really funny is, after time had passed and I had some distance from the situation, I would sometimes find out that the ex girlfriend had turned him into her "black hole of need"! He would follow her around like a little puppy dog hoping she would give him some attention. Who knew? Hilarious! I guess it's true about what goes around comes around. I kept thinking that there must be some trick that they knew that eluded me. Turns out the trick is called self-confidence. We as women have to find out who we really are and stay true to that. Then and only then will our true mate show up. Go figure.

Now, something I really find interesting about this time in my life is how much I grew in between each of my relationships. When I was alone, I was my true self and didn't have to pretend to be something I wasn't. Unfortunately, the time in between relationships was minimal. From the time I was sixteen, I was always beginning a relationship, in a relationship, or ending a relationship. I was continuously looking outside of myself for happiness. When I was in a relationship in those days, I wouldn't make any time for myself. Every waking moment, I was thinking about him and how I could make him happy. I was consumed with his needs above my own because I didn't know I had needs also, except of course, the need to be needed by him. I thought that was what I was supposed to do. That's was what the women of the time portrayed. Then after the break-up I would be devastated and I would have to find a way to get through my days again. Why? Because I had never developed my own life. I didn't have any interests or hobbies of my own that I enjoyed. So, when a man would end a relationship, the emptiness inside me felt like the size of the Grand Canyon. When they would leave, they would take with them everything that had consumed my days, so I would not only be alone again physically, but I was completely lost not knowing how to fill my days. Every activity was surrounding him and his interests.

Please let this be a little red alert for you ladies. If you have entered into a relationship with someone and you can't remember what you did with your day before he came into your life, you may be in trouble. You may be in danger of losing your identity. Don't worry. This is why you are reading this now. You are trying to change and grow and find out who you really are! That's huge!! Ask yourself the tough questions. Recognize if it is happening and do something about it. You may be in need of some serious girl time or some kind of outside activity that doesn't revolve around him. This is just something to keep in mind. Remember, "She Who Cares the Least Wins!" The more you care about your own needs for fulfillment, the more enticing you become to a man. After all, he has his own life and interests and so should you. He doesn't need a black hole of need sucking him dry! If you want to have a healthy relationship, knowing who you are and what you like is a must. Another huge rule is to never neglect your friendships with your girlfriends. They will always stick by you and shouldn't be ignored just because you have a new man in your life. There is nothing wrong with making sure your needs are met. You will win more of yourself if you keep who you are sacred. Think about what you would say to your best friend. Then remind yourself of the same thing. You have to be your own best friend.

I found, as I said earlier, that when I was forced to be alone, I really started to find myself and my own interests. Don't get me wrong, at first it wasn't easy. The first thing I would do after a break up is just lie on the couch feeling sorry for myself and eat every last grocery item in the fridge. Then, after some time had passed, I would realize I can't keep this up forever and that I would eventually have to do something that resembled living. So, I then move to the next step of grieving. I would get mad as hell and swear off men for good. I would tell myself that they are all pigs and I didn't need them. Believe it or not this really did help me to get my ass out of the house. Getting mad actually stirred up the energy to care about myself more than the jerk that left me. I knew that as bad as my heart was breaking it was still up to me to pull myself up out of the hole, put on my big girl panties. Even if you have the best friends in the world, it's still your choice how to move on in your life. I would tell myself I would be alright and after a while I would begin to believe it and feel better. Is this something you have experienced? We are not alone in our relationship experiences. All of us have a story to tell. Women have to learn to make themselves the first priority. You have to give yourself the love you want from others.

What really galls me about this phase in my life was the cycle that kept repeating. Just when I would finally get myself back together and I would begin to live my life again, another man would show up, or the ex would want me back. I would think to myself "GEEZ!! Are you kidding me GOD??" I couldn't see what I was doing. I would go from independent, confident women to clingy, black hole of need, then get dumped, then eventually back to independent, confident me again. I really tried to keep myself strong and balanced but I would always fall back into old habits. At first, when someone would ask me out on a date, I would pretend that I wasn't interested. Inevitably they would pursue me relentlessly. Crazy, isn't it? This is what I mean when I say, "She who cares the least wins"? If I seemed unobtainable I was like catnip to them and they had to have me. However, when I chased them they would bolt like a jack rabbit.

The same thing would happen over and over. After their relentless pursuit, I would believe their lies. I would succumb like a big dope and fall for all over again. Next step was to lose my identity and self confidence and become the black hole again, and of course they would run for the door. It's so amazing to think that what attracted men to me in the first place—appearance of confidence, my life, my interests and my hobbies—were the first thing that I would lose after entering into a relationship with them. I can't blame them for leaving me because, I portrayed being a confident, amazing woman and when that changed, then so did their attraction to me.

It was at this point in my mid-twenties that I decided I had had enough. I was not going to have another relationship until I could figure some things out about myself. I began by really starting to think about what I liked and didn't like doing and why did I like it? What really made me happy? Not what I had been told to like. Another thing I did was to start making "dates" for myself. I rented movies I wanted so see that maybe didn't interest anyone else. I also read only books that I found fascinating. I spent a lot of days pampering myself and asking questions like: What kind of life do I really want. What kind of man do I really want? What do I consider to be a healthy, happy relationship? What did it look like? Feel like? More importantly, I would question the images in my mind. Was it my idea or something manufactured by society? Sometimes I would ask more simple questions like: Am I feeling confident today? If not, why? I wrote lots of lists of things I wanted. I made journal entries to get my true feelings out and I cried when I felt like crying. No more apologies for being myself. When a man would ask me out and he wouldn't take no for an answer, I would lie and say I was seeing someone or that I was busy doing something else. I wouldn't accept their calls and if they were really relentless I would tell them that I was gay! That usually worked. After all, no one is going to have a sex change just for a date! Also, it didn't hurt that I had some wonderful friends that would back me up if I needed it. It's funny now to think of going to such extremes but I was all about self preservation back then. One thing (among many) that I wish men would understand is, if they see a group of women by themselves, it doesn't necessarily mean we are looking for male companionship. Sometimes, we just want to hang out and catch up with each other.

Anyway, I knew I had a lot of learning to do and I needed the time and space to do it. I must say that these days, I would probably handle the situation much differently. However, you do the best you can with what you know and move on as best you can. With time, I began to find that I really enjoyed spending time by myself and I would actually get a little perturbed when "my" time was interrupted. I turned down a lot of dates because I began to know instinctively that I wasn't ready yet and it would just be another disaster. I know that many of you hate the thought of being alone. Well, guess what? I found out that there is a big difference between being"alone" and being "lonely". If you don't love your own company and think you are a wonderful person, then how can anyone else ever love your company and also think you're fabulous? What would you do if you saw your best friend, wallowing in this black hole of pain, doubt and loneliness? What would you do for her? What would you say to her? Would you stand by and let it just continue? Well, you are your own best friend. You are the only one that knows what you need to hear, what you need to do to get out of that hole. Give yourself permission to care about your own needs so that you can develop your own potential. When you do, you will win back more of yourself. The world around you will get to see more of the amazing person you are. When you feel that pull to be sucked back into others' demands on you, say to yourself, "SHE WHO CARES THE LEAST WINS"! And RUN!!!!! It's not selfish to live up to your full potential. I believe it's what God wants us to do. I see it as just following orders from a higher source. What a great thing to do! There's no better time spent than the time spent in pursuit of being a better human being. You have wonderful gifts to share with the world, and the world is waiting.

The Chameleon

As I continued this journey of dissecting my behavior, I discovered that I also had a bad habit of being a chameleon. When I started to date someone, I would begin to lose what little identity I possessed. I would transform myself into whatever I thought the man wanted. I would ask endless questions of him and his friends and find out all of his interests, hobbies, etc. Then I *would* transform myself and pretend to be completely enthralled with everything they loved. Let me tell you, I was great at it. I didn't have any self identity, or hobbies or interests of my own so, it was easy to pretend to be something I wasn't, at least for a while. I never realized the extreme price I was paying. I was completely brilliant when I needed to play a role. I knew how to look pretty, wear the right clothes and play the part. It was my entire goal to make them want me, because then I would feel the love I craved. I never realized it was false love. They were attracted to what I was pretending to be, not the real me. Of course, I didn't know the real me so how on earth were they supposed to love me? I have watched endless sporting events which I hate. Listened to music I couldn't stand and even dressed in outfits I wouldn't be caught dead in just because he thought it looked good. I was desperate to be loved and accepted, but unwilling to give myself that same gift. Again, irony is so crazy in this world of self-discovery. I have dated jocks and nerds, bikers and musicians, professionals and blue-collar, etc. I tried every lifestyle you can imagine. Sometimes, I think I should have gone into acting, because, I could have won an academy award for "Best portrayal of a Girlfriend"!! Feeling better about your own dating life now? Great! Obviously the outcome was always the same because I couldn't maintain this fake identity indefinitely and he would eventually leave. With that being said, let's move on. Let us continue to forgive our past and grow into a phenomenal woman. It doesn't serve any purpose to beat yourself up. "The Past is nothing but the trail you leave behind you." Dr. Wayne Dyer.

From a very early age, most of us are taught to be caring and nurturing to others, but rarely taught to care for our own needs. I have already stated this previously but it bears repeating in order to GET YOU TO WAKE UP!!!! I'm not saying that caring for other isn't important. I definitely think that the world could use a lot more love and understanding. Although, what seems to happen to most of us is that we concentrate so much of our time on being the "good daughter, friend, sister, mother, girlfriend, or wife" that we forget to nurture and care for ourselves. Women play the roles very well, but most of the time they have no idea who they really are. The identity and self-esteem we should be developing takes a back seat to all the needs of others. After years of caring for others, we know exactly what they need and how to give it to them, but have little idea what we truly want or need. We change ourselves into whatever seems to be needed at the time.

In many relationships both with friends and boyfriends, I have found myself doing things I had zero interest in because I was afraid to say the word "no". I was so afraid that it might hurt someone's feelings or disappoint them. I was a chronic people pleaser. Instead of saying "no" like I wanted to I would let myself get talked into things and then resent both myself and them for the whole situation. What really makes me angry is that the whole time, I would beat myself up inside by thinking to myself. "How did I get into this situation? I really don't want to be here." I would be so angry with myself for not being stronger and voicing what I really wanted. How did this keep happening? Well, duh! DO I REALLY HAVE TO SAY IT AGAIN? It all stems from not knowing who I was as a woman and having a sense of self-worth. Ok, I think the point is really starting to get home. So, next epiphany I had on my journey was the deliberate manipulation by people around me.

Certain people can have dominating personalities and will spot the insecure, needy ones from a mile away and love exploiting them. They will say things like, "Oh come on it will be fun!" or "Please just do this for me and I'll do this or that for you later," which "later" never seemed to happen. Ask yourself if you are participating in any activities that do not interest you? If so, let me tell you that you are not alone! However, ask yourself why you are doing whatever it is that you don't want to do. Are you being manipulated like I was? Think about what you want to accomplish. Who do you really want to become? This is how I began to find a way out of being a doormat and stand up for myself. I think it might help you too. When someone asks you to do something that you really don't want to do, STOP. Take a breath. Most of the time the need is not immediate so DON'T give them an immediate answer! Say, "Hmmm, let me think about it and get back to you." Or, "I'm not sure right now, when do you need an answer?" This gives you time to decide what you want to do. I even wrote these statements on a piece of paper and kept them by the phone because I was a habitual "yes" girl. I would say yes and then beat myself up for not being stronger and saying no.

If this is you, I can relate and so can many of our sisterhood. If the person continues to ask you to commit after you have requested time think, let them talk, but realize that now they are trying to manipulate you to do what they want. You have to recognize that they are not hearing "NO". Now, it becomes your choice how you handle it. Keep repeating, "I understand what you're asking me but I'll have to get back with you when I'm sure." Or I have to check on some other commitments first. If this doesn't work, find a reason you have to hang up. Like, "I was just on my way out" etc. Do whatever it takes until you begin to find your voice to say no. No one can make you feel bad unless you let them. If you let them talk you down and you give in, then it's your fault and you will hate yourself for not being stronger. Only you can stand up for yourself. Only you can stop being walked on by other people. They won't stop until you make them stop.

We care way too much what other people think, instead of trusting our own opinions and feelings. I understand that you may not want to stand out from the crowd or voice your different opinion for fear of being ostracized or ridiculed. However, the only way to stop this manipulation is to start finding out who you really are and what you really want. When I say this to most women they give me a blank stare and say something like, "I never really thought about it," or, "I have never asked myself that before." Or the saddest answer of all, "I don't have time to think about what I want because I've got too much to do. Besides, don't you think that's selfish?" I tell them that the real crime is going through life never discovering the wonderful gifts you have to share with the ones you love. How will we begin to teach our daughters to value themselves if we don't learn to do it ourselves?

I knew something had to change, but I wasn't sure where to start. I asked myself, "How can I find out what I want and who I really am on the inside?" The first step I decided was to start to find out what did interest me? I really had no idea, so I started at a book store. A library is another great choice. When you look around at all of the different sections and categories I guarantee that you will find yourself drawn to certain areas more than others. Congratulations! You are on your way to finding out "who" you really are and what you are passionate about. When you begin to develop your own knowledge about something, then a kind of self confidence grows inside. Being confident in yourself and your abilities shows up like a bright light. Trust me on this. Knowledge is something which no one can ever take away from you. It's inside of you like a beacon. When you begin to find yourself, you will begin to get greedy for time alone so you can discover more. You will truly begin to be free. You will learn to really love who you are and people will want to be in your company. After all, if you don't enjoy your own company then how do you expect anyone else too? Who would you rather spend time with; a black hole of need, a chameleon, or a beacon of light and hope and a positive attitude? It doesn't matter where you start; it only matters that you start somewhere. It may be starting with a small herb garden or learning about a place that you want to travel to someday or even just a wonderful novel that you can escape into. It doesn't matter what it is as long as it's your decision what you want to do or learn about. Take a step in doing something, anything for yourself. I think you will like the change that begins to happen inside. Hobby stores are another wealth of ideas and opportunities to learn more about your interests and talents. When you get braver, try taking a class. It's a wonderful way to expand your horizons. Who knows where it could lead? Spending time with people of similar interests is a great self-esteem builder. The world is waiting to meet the real you. Real self-esteem doesn't happen overnight. It takes time, so be patient with yourself. Take baby steps and constantly explore your world. It is so worth the effort.

If you're still not convinced, think about this idea. Have you ever noticed that when you are in a relationship with someone, there seems to be an endless amount of men that are suddenly interested in you? However, when you're not involved you can't get a date to save your life. That's because of the energy you are sending out. When you are happy, content and perfectly confident in where you life is headed, you are sending out positive energy that is like a moth to a flame. When we are alone, all of our focus seems to turn to a desperation to have someone in our lives, even if it is Mr. Wrong. This sends out a signal to all men of "leech alert" beware! You will repel any and all relationships. Women have to learn to enjoy their own company and be comfortable with ourselves, with or without a man. This is your journey of self discovery. You have so much to offer the world. Now get busy girl!!

Ring Worthy or Fling Worthy?

So which one are you? Most think that they are definitely "Ring Worthy". However, your actions can be demonstrating the exact opposite. Men have a very exact definition of the women he will and won't take home to "Mother". I'm going to take you back in time for a bit to show how things have changed over the years. When I was growing up, it was a very big deal to stay a virgin until you were married. That was what young girls were told in traditional households. At the time though, the sixties had passed with the "sexual revolution" and women were exploring their own sexuality and needs. This I believe is where a lot of confusion of "do I" or "don't I" began. So many stigmas were attached if you weren't a virgin. God forbid if you were divorced or unfortunate enough to get pregnant. Then you were shipped off to "Aunt Edna's" where you would live in shame for your indiscretion and a story would be made up to explain your absence from the family. This was so sad and very difficult for women to endure. What I really despise is the fact that the man who was the co-conspirator walked away from the situation without any repercussions. Don't even get me started on men who don't take care of their responsibilities. Anyway, that's not what I want to address in this chapter.

What I want you to consider is the level of your personal power. Are you claiming it? Or are you giving it away? In the sixties there was a term called "Flower Power," which some said meant wishing a person inner peace. Others though seem to think it meant a women's gift of sex. I remember when I was young hearing the term "De-Flowering". I had no idea what it meant and thought it rather ridiculous. How can you de-flower a flower? It exists and can't just disappear or go away once it's there alive and growing. Later of course, I came to understand this meant losing your virginity. So, that got me to thinking. Why over many generations a flower has been used to symbolize a women's sexuality? I think there is a lot of power in this example. For instance, a flower starts as a small bud then matures into a full bloom and only when it is ready does it open itself up to its full glory. I can easily see the similarity to women. We also start small then slowly develop into women and then when we are ready we give what some consider their most sacred gift, their virginity. There can be only one first! I realize that this sounds extremely old fashioned but I ask you to just think about it for a minute.

A women's "virginity" as well as the act of making love can be a powerful and intimate gift and shouldn't be taken lightly. To open yourself up literally and physically to a man puts you at your most vulnerable.

You are traditionally on your back, belly exposed. Which, even to animals this is the way they show submission to others. You are physically trusting and surrendering yourself underneath him. Don't you think that this trust and surrender to a man should be earned? I do!

Just like the flower on the vine, as long as it's attached it lives and thrives. When you pick a flower, it immediately begins to die without the connection to its source of life. It can survive if it is nourished by food and water but it must be cared for by another. You have to decide who is worthy of such an important gift. So, using this analogy, think about your relationships. If you wait for sex until you choose to be ready, you keep the power of that life as well as the control over it being nurtured. When you give it up there is a chance that you will not be cared for but left to your own demise. It should be a decision that you make with great care. I have no doubt you or someone you know has experienced this situation. I'm not saying you should never give in but you have to decide who will have the power, you or him? You should always be in charge of what happens to your body! I suggest trying one simple test.

When you are with a man and you are considering taking it to the next level, look him directly in the eyes. Ask yourself one very important question. "Do I believe that he will still be with me when I give in or will he bolt now that he got what he wanted?" If there is

ANY doubt, don't do it. It's really that simple. Doubt means don't. That's why God gave us gut instincts. They never lie to us. When you don't listen, it always comes back to bite you and then you beat yourself up for not listening. If he leaves you because you won't sleep with him, then you know for sure that sex was all he wanted. Trust me real men will put in the time if they consider you "Ring Worthy". Otherwise you are just "Fling Worthy" and he will hit the ground running as soon as he can put his shoes on. Over the years I have interviewed many men on this subject and without fail they all agree on the basics about women. Of course they want to sleep with every women they can, that's a given. They are hunters and love the chase. One thing you must understand though is the only women that they will marry and commit to are the ones that have dignity, integrity, and most of all have high self-esteem. This information comes directly from the horse's mouth so to speak. They believe that if you will go to bed with them so easily then you will go to bed with all men that easily. They do not want someone that every man has had before them. That is not what they consider "Ring Worthy". Even though a man says he "loves you", "respects you" etc., that may or may not be a "Guy Lie" which I will cover in another chapter. So let them prove their desires are real. If a vow of monogamy or commitment hasn't been established, then you are setting yourself up for a major disappointment. Trust me on this; it comes straight from men themselves. You give the flower; you lose the power and are vulnerable to the outcome he chooses. Do you really want to be put in that position?

Decide for yourself what you will and won't put up with from men. Commit to yourself to hold yourself to a higher standard. I have heard some women say that this is too hard and that they will be sitting home alone. I disagree. What you put out you will get back. Let's take a look at the most blatant, example of this I can think of, women in Hollywood. Think about actresses like Julia Roberts, Reese Witherspoon, Queen Latifah, Beyonce, Hillary Swank, Oprah Winfrey, Katie Holmes. I could go on but that's enough to get the point. All of these women are exposed to the same Hollywood industry and scrutiny. However, you don't see them running around sleeping with everyone, making sex tapes, in and out of drug rehabs or Showing off to the world the fact that they aren't wearing panties. You all know the other women I am referring too. I'm sure I don't need to name names. All of the women I previously mentioned have been or are in monogamous relationships that required a higher level of respect and commitment. Of course, these are all just my opinion based on the example they seem to portray. You are the only one that gets to decide what kind of woman you want to become. If you want a jerk, there are plenty out there. If you want a real man then hold yourself to a higher standard and the "real" men will show up. If you don't feel your self-esteem is where it should be or don't feel worthy of the great men out there, then definitely you don't need to be dating until you have done some serious self-analysis. Your image is critical to getting what you want out of any relationship. If you settle for less, then there is no one to blame but yourself. I believe all women deserve to be treated with respect, love and kindness. You don't have to be a "Bitch" but you do have to be a "Lady" in order to be treated like one. "Now" is always the best place to begin because the past is over and the future is yet to be determined. Every moment is a new moment and an opportunity to begin again. Take a good look at yourself and continue to focus your attention on the woman you want to become. Don't beat yourself up if you lose your power and slide back into old habits every now and then. Just pick yourself up and start over.

You are Valuable and Precious

N ow that you have some idea of how you have been programmed by outside influences, it's up to you what you choose to do with this new knowledge. My hope is that you continue your journey with a new awareness; and with this new awareness you will choose your own beliefs above those of others. After all, this is your journey through life, your path, and only you can take the next step to achieving your goals. Only you know what is best for you.

So, how do we begin to value ourselves? First, as I mentioned in the previous chapters, find out what your interests are and pursue them. Be voracious about finding your interests as you have been about finding "The One". Find others who share the same interest because it strengthens friendships and builds lasting relationships. Take a really good look at what and who is in your environment. Are you surrounded with positive, uplifting things and people? Or is your world a mixture of depressing and negative things and people. This is critical to changing your view of the world. If you are engulfed in negativity then it's no wonder you are alone. Negative environments breed negative outcomes. This includes what you watch, read and the home you live in. You must start every day thinking about the positive things in your life. You must live in a state of gratitude in order to bring more things to be grateful for.

Next, I want you to do something for me. I want you to get up and go to a mirror. Get close to it and look yourself directly in the eye. I know you might feel silly but trust me this is important. Now, tell me what you see. What are you saying to yourself right now? Whatever you tell yourself in this moment is what you're reflecting and putting out to the world. Don't believe me? Think about your life. How are your relationships? How is your work environment? What about your overall health? Are they great? Then terrific! Or could they be better? If you are not feeling particularly friendly towards yourself right now that's ok. However, let's get busy and start to change it. I want you to look in the mirror again and say five things that you like about yourself, OUT LOUD! For instance, I have pretty eyes, or I am a good person, or I am really good to my pets. It doesn't matter what the five things are, what matters is the shift in your mind set that has now occurred. Be sure to say them with real feelings, not just hollow words. That doesn't achieve the same goal. When you begin to feel better about yourself, a change happens in your brain. An actual chemical change begins to take place and this reaction resonates through your whole body. The longer you can hold on to this good feeling the more reaction will occur and the more you can build on the positive things about yourself. You will begin to feel it throughout your body. Then maybe you will begin to value the precious gift that you are and the world will respond. I recommend saying at least one positive affirmation about yourself every morning when you begin your day. Learn to love yourself one bit at a time. This will begin a ripple effect of appreciation for yourself and all you have to offer.

Here are a couple of things I do with when I am having a difficult time feeling good about myself. First get busy! Get up off the chair or couch and move. Exercise, even housework, has been proven to release tension and help relieve depression. Quit the self destructive pattern of "poor me" or "I can't do it". It is critical to feel good about yourself as much as humanly possible, throughout the day, until it becomes a natural state of being. Sometimes, I will start by doing something for myself on the outside to change my mood. It might be buying nail polish or lipstick. It might be listening to my favorite music blasting or maybe I will soak in a hot bubble bath. My point is that it doesn't really matter what turns the tables for you, but it is important to make that turn. What you like and enjoy is what makes you unique. There is only one you and you are very important. You are completely different than everyone else in the universe. Cherish this fact and make a commitment to be the best you possible. When you spend all of your time caring for and about others, how long do you think you will last?

The well will eventually run dry and you can't give what you don't have. You have to find a way to give yourself love and fill up the well inside you in order to give back to the world. We have to find ways of keeping the outside and inside in a positive equal amount of energy.

Another trick that has really worked for me is the use of Vision Boards. If I don't have one handy, I will sometime just close my eyes and visualize something beautiful. For instance it could be a sunset on the beach, a walk in woods or even your favorite food. It always helps me to get back into a positive frame of mind quicker than anything else. I try to keep pictures all around that immediately evoke a positive feeling so that I can stay focused when I need it. I think this is one of the easiest things for someone to do to change the way they feel inside. Even "Oprah" puts a page in every issue of her magazine called "Breathing Space". The entire page is a photograph specifically chosen to bring forth a feeling of awe, wonder, and peace. The pictures are always amazing and I look forward to them in every issue. There must be something to it if Oprah does it right? If you don't have any pictures then start with some magazines that you can cut out images, or get a calendar with pictures you love. The library or internet are wonderful sources for photographs that inspire you. After you have assembled your favorite images, cut them out and put them where you can see them every day. You can keep them in a folder, tape them to your mirror or better yet, attach them to a big poster board that can hang up and pass by on a regular basis. I believe tremendously in vision boards. Little by little your attitude will begin to change because of the change you made in your environment and what you have chosen to focus on. Nothing happens overnight, it takes time, so be patient with yourself. Don't beat yourself up. That's a waste of spirit and time. Alright, now that we have some skills to work on the inside, it's time to work on the outside

I think our outside appearance is as important for our self-esteem as the inside view of ourselves. I want to be very clear here. I'm not talking physical body appearance. That's on a different level all together than what I am referring to. It doesn't matter what you weigh or look like, for the time being. There are other issues going on there. I'm talking wardrobe, honey. If you think that clothes don't make the woman, then let me tell you: you're wrong. What you wear can suck the life out of you. I realize that this will seem like a very superficial thing considering we are supposed to be fixing the inside feelings; however, I assure you that this is directly related. Let me give you an example of what I mean. Picture yourself in sweat pants, a T-shirt that might even be stained and tube socks or flip flops. Your hair is undone and your face hasn't seen make-up for days. Boy! Aren't you a gorgeous creature? Do you feel beautiful, attractive, like a sex goddess? I doubt it.

Now, the reason I purposely chose this image is because I want you to really feel how this appearance makes you feel inside. Comfortable, sure, but this attire can affect your self-esteem and so therefore affects how value yourself. I'm not saying that sweats aren't an essential part of your wardrobe but keep them for cleaning the house or working out at the gym. Otherwise, get yourself dressed everyday in real clothes. There are so many wonderful casual affordable clothes out there that are cute and fit any size. Use accessories to spruce it up a bit. Do your hair and make-up. Please, don't be the example caught out in public in the fashion "DON'T" section. I can't imagine how embarrassing that would be for someone. Of course, If they cared more they wouldn't be in that section. Case closed. If you don't value your appearance, then no one else will either.

Now, let's look at the opposite scenario. I want you to think about a time when you got dressed up and were feeling great. This doesn't necessarily have to mean wearing an evening gown, it could be a great pair of jeans and nice blouse or dress shirt; it doesn't matter. I want you to see yourself clearly in the mirror. Your clothes fit perfectly, your make-up and hair are flawless and you know you have it going on. How does this make you feel inside by comparison? I know you can see and feel the difference in the two scenarios immediately. So, what I'm getting at is the time and effort you put into your outer appearance can directly affect how you feel about yourself on the inside. That directly affects how you value yourself. Get it? Of course you do. By the way you choose to dress, you state to everyone around you how you feel about yourself. Sometimes though, you have to fake it until you feel it. I'm not saying that you must dress up every day and that everything needs to be perfect in order to feel good. However, I do expect you to care enough about yourself to shower, brush your teeth, comb you hair. etc., and put on something that will help you get into a better frame of mind and use your images to round out your feelings. OK? What I do believe is that when you care about your appearance it changes your attitude, and this new attitude reflects to the world a sense of confidence and self worth. The positive energy that you begin to send out will bring more opportunities to value yourself. Soon the world will have to step up its game to match the self confidence that you now exude. You have to begin to care for and about yourself if you ever want anyone else too. Start out small and build it more every day. Get your nails done, hair done etc. Do something for yourself. It's not selfish, it's required. Start to care more about yourself and others will see your confidence level rise. They will probably start asking you what you are doing differently. Start to care less what others think and more what you decide is your truth. Remember, I'll say it again, "She who cares the least wins!"

Guy Lies and Manipulations

I really wish that this was a chapter that I didn't have to write. I wish I could say that all men were truthful and honorable; however, if you are over the age of ten, you have probably already experienced a lie or manipulation by a man. I do want to firmly state that there are some men that are truthful and honorable. Unfortunately, is seems even the best of men can succumb to their basic animal instincts on occasion. When it comes to the issue of a man wanting to have sex, they can be extremely deceptive and downright manipulative. It really doesn't matter why they lie or manipulate. However, I think women need a real heads up at least as far as some basics. I believe women not only need to recognize the "lies" but be ready with a quick and definitive response to let the man know immediately that she is no fool and he had better step up his game in order to be with her.

After talking to women and men, I found there are many "lies" and manipulations" to address them all, so, I'm only going to cover some of the big ones. Once you read through these you will recognize enough patterns to be able to defend yourself easily and come up with other responses.

The first lie, I remember was when I was first beginning to date. The evening had gone very well and he was taking me home. We pulled in the drive way and my heart was pounding. It had come time for the good night kiss. At first I wasn't even sure he was going to get a kiss. I was face to face with a huge dilemma. He was very persistent so I gave in and we shared a very nice, very long kiss. Then I could see that the kiss had gotten him very aroused and he said, "It's your fault I got all excited, you have to fix it or it will be painful for me." WOW! Really??? What exactly did he expect me to do in my driveway? I told him I was sorry and bolted for the door. I felt bad for weeks and felt very embarrassed and guilty. I realize now I was so naïve. First of all, it absolutely isn't your fault in any way. A man can get an erection anytime, anywhere and for any number of reasons. He can also lose it just as fast with NO pain just by thinking of anything displeasing to him. So ladies, the next time a guy tries to feed you this load of crap look him dead in the eye and say, "I can't believe you really think I'm that stupid!" Say it with complete contempt and disgust and that he would think you would accommodate him. The other alternative which I personally like: Offer him a small bottle of hand lotion from your purse and tell him to go home and take care of it himself! I'm sure he has more practice than you do anyway! Then kick his butt to the curb! You deserve better than that Jack ass.

The next "Guy Lie" or manipulation I remember came when I was in college. It's the often used, "If you loved me you would—." Fill in the blank because this one can be used for anything from have sex with me, or allowing him to do something you don't want him to do. For instance, go to a strip club with the guys. The best response for this so far seems to be what I call the flip and reverse. "If you loved me you wouldn't ask—" again fill in the blank. Normally, he will realize that this argument is completely useless. Sometimes, however they will persist with this futile argument. If he does not take no for an answer, this is your cue that he has now moved into trying to manipulate you by making you feel bad or guilty. He may try badgering, nagging and even sometimes pouting like a child. Stand your ground or you will forever be a doormat for this logic. What I really find hilarious about this particular kind of "manipulation" is men don't realize they are completely out-matched. When it comes to badgering, nagging, or pouting to get something we want, women are masters. Women have spent generations perfecting this manipulation on men and are highly skilled. I always have to giggle whenever a girlfriend tells me about some man she dated and his lame attempts to manipulate her.

The next big lie I encountered was after I was out of college and working in the real world. I call it the "She's just a friend" lie. The men at this stage in my life were more of a marrying age and this bought up a whole new set of problems, When a man says this to you, it is possible it is absolutely true. However, it can also be his way of keeping one in the wings just in case it doesn't work out with you. This one can be a very tricky situation and you should proceed with caution. If it is true and she really is a friend, you could ruin a wonderful relationship from unsubstantiated paranoia. On the other hand, if it's more than friendship then you end up feeling incredibly stupid and naïve for not recognizing the truth. If this happens to you, and you do end up getting fooled, this has nothing to do with you. He is the "jerk;" don't stop trusting your instincts because he lied. That's on him and his character as a man, not you. Trust me they always get it back in the end. Move on, and be grateful he will never be able to do that to you again. So, what is the best way to know if she really is just a friend? First, trust your gut at all times. Always remember this! Your head is too logical, your heart is too emotional; it's your gut that is your source of truth. If it's twisting when she is around, and it didn't before, then that may be something to pay attention to. Second, has his behavior changed since she came into the picture? Is he dressing different? Has he started grooming himself more? An absolute dead giveaway is if he talks about her nonstop and her name keeps coming up all the time. This can be cause for alarm and time to question him further about the relationship with this woman. Finally, I believe the biggest clue is if you are not invited to meet her and you are never invited to come along and go with them to lunch, etc. These are just a few main ones to watch for; however, I still think there is no better signal than your gut. Trust it because it never lies to you.

Now, because there seems to be a lot of "Guy Lying" going on, it could be really easy to get jaded and feel like you can't trust any man. I understand, but an important point to consider is—you wouldn't want to pay for the mistakes his ex made, nor be compared to her right? So, don't do the same to a new potential mate. Take him for face value until he shows you otherwise. Many women ruin a possible great relationships because of suspicion without any facts whatsoever, and that's really sad. Meanwhile, a great guy is left wondering, "Wow what the hell happened to her? " Jealousy and suspicion are lousy ways to proceed in a relationship. If you can't get past it just now then maybe you should consider taking yourself off the market until you can resolve it. Everyone deserves a fresh start and a new beginning.

Another little gem which I and other women have heard over the years is the infamous, "I'm going to leave my wife. It's just complicated." First of all, if he hasn't left her yet, then more than likely he will never leave her. There is never a good reason to even consider pursuing this relationship. Never date a married man. It can only end in heartache. Turn, run and don't look back. When a man is truly done in a relationship, he's out of there. There isn't anything that will keep him. Besides, the obvious fact that if he is married and has you as his mistress, then why would he need to give one up? He will continue to keep you twisting in the wind as long as possible. Don't be naïve, ladies. When you finally do wake up and leave, he will just find someone else to lie to. Dating a married man is NEVER a good thing to do. No exceptions. This lie actually leads me to another lie I have heard women talk about which is, "My wife and I don't have sex anymore." This is used for one reason and one reason only. To elicit sympathy or pity from women in the hope that she will give him sympathy or pity sex. He doesn't care how he gets laid, just that he gets laid. That's his whole agenda and he will say whatever it takes to get the prize. This is one of the most insidious of all lies. Men know that women, by nature, are care givers and nurturers, so it really burns my butt that a man will use this wonderful trait in women to exploit. Beware of the man trying to play on your sympathy. He absolutely does not need to be talking to you about his personal relationship with his wife even if this is true. You need to tell him that the only person he should be talking to about his sexual relationship is his wife. If he can't resolve the issue with her, then he needs to seek counseling, but that will not be coming from you because you do not get involved with married men.

One of my all time favorites is the most popular lie, "My wife and I are separated." Before you even consider dating this man find out everything you can about him. Be a complete blood hound and leave no question unanswered. When he says that they are "separated" does that mean she's just not with him in the room at the moment or he has moved out of the home? If he is living in his own place, how long has been there? How long has he been separated and when will the divorce be final? If it is a recent separation or if he can't tell you when the divorce will be granted then, again, I say RUN!!! The reason you need to be so inquisitive is that up to seventy percent of men that are separated go back to their wives. I found out that statistic from a divorce attorney whom had seen it time and again. Just because he is separated, don't be too sure that he is really ready to move on with a new relationship. Unless he is divorced for sure and the relationship with his ex is really over, I wouldn't waste another breathe, much less my time and possibly my heart. This is a good time to implement the "Catch and Release" program. He might be great, but not just yet. You caught him, looked him over and changed your mind, so throw him back in the pond and walk.

There are many other lies that men use like, "I'll call you and we will get together" and they never do call. I detest this one because I would much rather them say, "Nice to meet you" and move on. To imply that he is going to take some action to pursue a relationship and then doesn't just leaves us twisting in the wind. The one similar to this is, "I was too busy to call." This makes me furious! I'm supposed to believe that in the past twenty four hours you couldn't find thirty seconds to just let me know you were thinking of me? With our multiple avenues of communication that has to be the biggest load of crap ever and, worse, it implies that we are so gullible that we would believe that load of bull!

I'll tell you one of the biggest truths about men. If a man wants to be with you, He will make it happen. I have dated some extremely busy men in my life and they ALWAYS found a way to get to me when they wanted to. There isn't anything that will deter his pursuit. They will find a way to call, text, e-mail, My Space, Twitter, Face book and so on, even if it is only for a moment. If he isn't calling you regularly and often just to hear your voice, then forget him and move on. He's not going to call. Save yourself the heartache and wasted energy. My stepsister had a wonderful saying about men which I will share with you to help this really sink in. Men are like Kleenex's. You take one from the box, use it as you please, then throw it away when you're done. Then, look! There's another one in its place! It's like magic. I know, I know that's an awful thing to say, but you have to keep a sense of humor, otherwise you can drive yourself crazy over thinking things. I love men and I love my husband deeply, but they can be a real pill sometimes and we need to keep a little ammo in our pockets. So, relax, have a little fun in your life. Don't take yourself so seriously. At least now you have an arsenal of ideas and comebacks against "Guy Lies and Manipulations".

The Observation

In college, I began to question everything around me. I was going through some major changes and I became absolutely fascinated with human behavior, especially women's behavior because after all I am one. Why did we act the way we did? Why do we get all goofy when it comes to having relationships with men? Why were women so mean to each other? This fascination would later lead me to my bachelor's degree in psychology. I didn't realize at the time, but I began a life long journey of self-examination and analysis as well as observing human behavior. I began to learn more about myself and my patterns of behavior; I was able to observe the similarities in other women. Unfortunately, I still had a lot to learn and I got my heart broken many times from repeated behavior. This is how I discovered "The Black Hole Syndrome" and how I would turn into a "Chameleon" instead of being myself. Like most people in their twenties, I liked going out on the weekends dancing with my friends and, of course, meeting men. Sometimes there would be hook-ups with men and sometimes not. I was just doing what most twenty-something's did on the weekend. Of course, when there would be hook-ups for myself or my friends, it would usually end in disaster. I would wonder what happened. I couldn't quite figure it out at the time. So I would shake it off and repeat the behavior. After too many one night stands and more bad relationships than I care to remember, I finally got a clue. I decided to step back and take a closer look at who I really was as a woman. I remember saying to myself, "What the hell am I doing?" This is when I decided to stop dating altogether until I could figure out why I kept trying so hard to be loved by men. I also got the idea for a study in the mating dance of men and women. The big question was, how was I going to learn from my mistakes without making them over and over? Simple, I would watch everyone else make the mistakes and pay attention and try to get a clue what was happening!!! You would think that most of the things that I am going to tell you would be obvious, but for me it was anything but obvious. I became a voyeur/investigator. I began asking all these questions and wondering "why" about everything. I had endless discussions with my friends about their relationships, only to end up with more questions. I decided that I had to approach this endeavor completely different.

The first thing I had to do was find a target rich environment to observe as many people as possible. I also had to do this without them knowing that I was observing them. As luck would have it at the time, my sister was working her way through college as a bartender at one of the more popular nightclubs in town. Was that perfect or what? For the next three months every Friday and Saturday night I would sit at the end of the bar from open to close and watch. I would watch the parade of people come through the door and pick certain ones to observe for the evening. It never ceased to amaze me what some of the people would come in wearing and I'm not being mean. If you have been out in the last twenty years you know exactly what I'm talking about. Let's just say that I think some things should be left to the imagination. Now, having an inside track on certain clientele from my sister definitely helped in the study. She knew all the regulars as well as who was there for fun and who was there for covert operations. We even had all of these unspoken hand signals to point out different types of people. Without saying a word she could shoot me a look with certain understood hand jesters and I would know immediately what to look for. The signals were very much like using your first finger and thumb to represent "loser" but much more subtle.

This is what I discovered. There are basically three types of people that go to the night club scene. The first type I call the "Pro". This is normally a man, but on occasion, I have seen women also portray this to perfection. They would be your typical "Gold Digger". This is the person that is perfectly dressed. They look and smell great. I often found myself wondering how much time these individuals took to get that perfect. Unfortunately, this is where perfection ends. The problem with the "Pro" or "Gold Digger" is that they are always out for the hook up. No long term commitments are desired. They usually only want a one night stand unless they deem you worthy of further abuse and you decide to sign up for it. These are the ones that are dangerous and shallow and are to be avoided at all cost. They will tell you everything you want to hear and will have you believing that they are God's gift sent just for you. If he seems too perfect, sister, you had better stand back and take a better look. On second thought RUN!

The second type is the fun, outgoing, party people. These are the groups of people that just love to get together and hang out. They come in like a blaze of glory, very lively and joyous. This group is full of life. They seem to be experiencing the world like those wonderful vacation ads. Everyone is having a great time at amazing parties. They are really oblivious to anyone else there, because they are having so much fun in their own little group. I was always very envious of these people. I wanted to be included in their fun. They reminded me of the T.V. show, *Friends*. They come in and leave together always having a wonderful time talking and dancing. They were the most fun to watch.

The last and final group of people I call the "targets". These poor people will come in and immediately start scanning the room looking for their "Mr. or Ms. Right". You can see it in the way they are trying so hard to be perfect. They usually primp a lot or just seem a little uncomfortable. They are so desperate to be noticed that their actions are normally over exaggerated. They become very animated and want desperately to be the life of the party. Or they will sink into a spot and just constantly scan the room hoping someone will approach them. I'm sure you have heard the term "Wall Flower". You can feel the painful desperation oozing out of them. The ones that over exaggerate are also the people that you will see stripping their off clothes or dancing on the tables to get noticed. These people truly break my heart. I have to confess though, that in my past, I had moments when I was this poor deluded person. Live and learn baby, live and learn. At the conclusion of my study I made a very sad discovery. The scenario that played out most of the time was this: "Pro" would hook up with a "Target" and the party people left together. I always felt so bad for the "Target" but we all have to learn on our own.

I began this study to learn about myself, but it also helped to further my degree in Psychology and human studies in general. However, after months of observation, I had another amazing epiphany. All of these character traits are in all of us but we portray different ones at different times throughout our lives. In every imaginable situation throughout the day, I could see people acting like these funny little stereotypes I had created in my head. The "Pro", the "Party People," and the "Targets" were everywhere. It was really quite fascinating.

Sometimes, I would be in the corporate world watching the interaction between colleagues, then in a grocery store observing the looks as people would pass each other. Even out with friends at a park or in the gym working out. I couldn't believe I never recognized this before. I had been so completely self- absorbed in my own little world. I had never paid attention to the world around me. It turns out that the people around me were just as big a mess inside their heads. All this time I thought it was just me and everyone else had it all together. What a great feeling to know I wasn't alone.

I highly recommend the next time you are at work or just running errands, try to see how many of the three types you can spot. You probably won't even have to leave your house to imagine a few stand outs you already know in your life. Next, ask yourself the more important question which one you're portraying. Then ask, "Is that really who you want to show to the universe?" I promise you will get what you ask for in this world.

One thing I know for sure, as "Oprah" says, is that your life is the way it is because of the choices you have made throughout your life. If your life is not what you want, then there is no one else to blame but you, so quit wasting time and energy blaming everything and everyone else. The good news is that, because it's your choice, you can change your life and any situation by making the choice to do it. The Universe has a bigger dream for you than you can ever imagine. However, sometimes you have to get out of your own way and let the Universe do its' work. Quit trying to be God in your own life; trust me you aren't good at it. Instead, every day, say out loud what you want, write out in detail what you want and then be open to every opportunity that presents itself. Start saying "yes" to things even if you're scared. Life has a way of working things out, even when you are in the way of progress. You are an amazing person so why not let it come out and be the person you always knew your true self to be? Quit listening to what other people tell you to do or how you are supposed to be in this world. No one knows your dreams better than you! So, I'll say it again, "She who cares the least wins!" Take care of yourself and your personal needs first and you will have more of your true self to give back to the world.

Why Doesn't He Get Me?

Communication differences between men and women have been an issue since time began. Men and women's brains are hardwired completely differently, and this can cause major communication breakdowns between the sexes. One problem is women are much more verbal than men. Studies have shown women on average use two to three times more words in day as opposed to men. Women want men to understand and to hear us, but what we tend to do is hit him with a verbal barrage when a simple sentence is all that is needed. The poor man is trying to understand and give us what we want, but all Men hear is the "teacher's voice" from Charlie Brown. You know the one I'm talking about. Charlie Brown says something and the teacher's answers in garbled sounds "WARH WAH... WARH, WARH, WARH." I'm not sure there is an exact answer to this communication problem, but here is a suggestion: when a man comes through the door after a long day, give him some space to decompress. He doesn't need you to blast him with the thousands of words you haven't used for the day. He can't take in everything you're saying because he is in "information overload". Secondly, if he is quiet and seems distant, don't take it personally; he has more than likely, exceeded his daily allowance of words at work and is just done for the day. Just accept his one word responses and move on or wait for a later time to engage him in conversation. He will be much more responsive if he has some down time. I have discovered a few other insights that will help you understand how men and women think differently. Hopefully, these insights will help clear up some of the mystery. Studies have also been done which prove men and women think differently when it comes to problem solving. It's not just our imaginations.

Men tend to be very linear thinkers, while women are more abstract thinkers. In other words, men think: A, B, C, D, E, F, then the problem is solved. Women, on the other hand, think more like: C, A, D, F, B, E, then their problem is solved. Even though the end result is the same, the approaches are completely opposite. If you have ever worked on a project with a man, then you probably are having flash backs of a disaster that took place. Both of you are right; it's just different. I suggest that, in the future, if you are going to work on any project with a man, before you begin, decide who is going to be in charge and then stick to it.

My husband and I have found over the years that there are "territories" that we have to defer to each other. For instance, anything in the garage or that has do to with building or fixing something is definitely my husband's area of expertise. However, when it comes to cooking, housework, decorating, etc, that is my territory. There are sometimes when we cross over, but for the most part we stick to what we do best. Most people consider this type of relationship traditional, maybe even old fashion, but it works for us. My point is, you really need to discuss what works best for both of you and then learn to defer to each other. He might be the better cook and you might be a better builder, doesn't matter, if it works for the two of you.

Another huge difference women need to understand is: men are black and white when it comes to communication. Women, however, are multiple shades of gray. When you are trying to get your point across to a man it's really very simple. Say what you mean and state what you want. Men don't like or understand metaphors, euphemisms, or sarcasm. They really wish you would just get to the point. Going on and on complaining drives them crazy; it is a complete waste of time and it never works. Before you talk to a man about an issue that's bothering you, think about the main point you want make and leave out the rest of the conversation. He loves you and wants to make you happy, but you have to be clear when stating your needs. Be simple and direct and make the request in black and white. This approach he will respect and appreciate. Don't waste his time and yours, and don't give him attitude or it will blow up in your face.

Also, always select a neutral time to talk. Do not choose a time when he is engrossed in something like the Super bowl or when the conversation gets heated! If you don't remember anything else from this chapter, remember this! When you want to discuss something, NEVER say, "We need to talk." This simple statement puts everyone on the defensive including women. It's like being called to the principal's office. Everyone knows when they hear, "We need to talk;" it means, "oh man, I did something wrong and I'm in trouble!!!" Men hate this statement because it is always followed by how they screwed up again in your eyes. No one likes to disappoint someone or be made to feel like they don't measure up to someone's expectations. They will immediately feel defeated and they will not hear whatever it is you are trying to say. Instead a much nicer, softer approach is asking him, "Honey, can we visit for a minute? I want to ask/tell you something." You can put it in your own words of course but I think you get my point. Try not to come off like you're on the attack and you will have a much healthier discussion. Get to the point.

Another communication mistake I see women make all of the time is what I call "Tone Assumptions". A man will say "Hello" and in their minds they think, "What did he mean by that." We are very sensitive to tone of voice, often too sensitive. If he is smiling and very upbeat then we relax, if he is quieter and distant we panic. We immediately, "Assume" it has something to do with us. In our minds, we start the drilling of questions. "What did I do? Was it something I said? Is he mad at me? Oh no! Does he still love me? Does he want to break up with me?" GEEZ LADIES! All he said was "Hello" and your little monkey mind went bouncing off of the walls. If you don't act like this, then I guarantee you know a woman who does.

Let me tell you exactly what he meant when he said "Hello"..........He meant...... "Hello". That's it, plain and simple!! Nothing else entered his mind, I promise. As I stated before, men are black and white. If they have a problem with you, they will eventually tell you. This observation leads me to the next issue, which is how men and women are different when it comes to solving an external problem. I'm going to use relationship issues as an example since that is what we really want to understand. Let's say a man is having problem with his girlfriend/spouse. First, he will want to be completely alone. He doesn't want to discuss it in any way, shape or form. He likes, being alone with his thoughts to sort things out without any interruptions. If you badger him by constantly asking him if anything is wrong, it will only aggravate the situation. Leave him alone to figure it out. Next, if he has exhausted every scenario in his mind and can't find a solution, only then he will ask advice from you or others. This is a last resort. Men like to work things out for themselves. They are usually very private about their emotions, so respect that and leave them alone. If you know for sure that something is bothering them, then ask them once if you can help. If they say no then drop it. Just tell him, "I'm here if you want to talk about it." This approach goes over much better than badgering. We know we just want to help but that isn't the way it comes across. Instead of nurturing them, it's smothering them. Most of all, try not to assume it's all about you. He could be having a problem with a co-worker, boss, friend, relative, etc. It could be that or he is just tired or is disappointed his team lost. Instead make this assumption. If you don't know for sure it is about you, then "ASSUME" it's not until you find out otherwise! There, problem solved.

Now, as for women, the absolute opposite is true. If we are having a problem with our significant other we will exhaust ourselves and everyone around us discussing it. We will ask our mothers, girlfriends, guy friends, neighbors, hairdresser, local butcher, grocery store clerk, bank teller, and, in general, anyone who lends us an ear. If this doesn't solve the problem to our satisfaction, then we will then go into major research mode. We will read every magazine article, book, or pamphlet we can get our hands on. We will watch videos on the subject or go online to chat rooms and talk until we are blue in the face. When the hunt for answers has been completely beaten to death, we then compile all of the data and make our decisions. I do find this funny because I still do this too. I know what my gut says but it's so nice to have reassurance I'm doing the right thing from my surrounding universal little family. I don't think it's because we think others know more or what is best for us. I think we just like to hear that our instincts are right and valid. There is a wonderful visual that I think will help explain just how different men and women's brain really are. Picture a women's brain like a high tech, complicated intricate, machine. There is an elaborate mass of wires, switches, cables, pulleys, buttons, levers, knobs and an alarming number of flashing lights. In contrast the man's brain is an on/off switch. I am NOT saying that men are not intelligent. Bill Gates…..hello? All I am saying is we are different, and understanding this fact will help when you are trying to get your point across.

Finally, a big issue women need to understand is men are "Fixers". If you start talking about a problem you are having, his brain immediately goes into trying to find a solution. He thinks you are telling him the problem so that he can "fix it" (switch on). When you don't take his advice, he can get extremely frustrated. In his mind, he is thinking, "Why did she even tell me the problem if she refuses to take my advice?" (switch off). Women don't understand why he is upset because we were just venting. Most of the time, women already know what they are going to do; they just want to gripe about it for a while to get it off their chest. Then we feel better and can go on about our day. The man is left dumbfounded and confused. Here is how you can avoid this miscommunication. If you are having a problem and you want to talk about it make it clear up front if you are just "venting" or if you want him to give you the answer to "fix it". Tell him, "I have an issue I would like your input on", or, "Honey, I don't need you to 'fix it' but I just need to vent and have you listen." This will prevent the communication problem before it occurs.

So, in conclusion, I don't think there is anything wrong with women needing a sounding board or men needing to go off alone to figure it out. Neither approach to problem solving is wrong; it's just different. Understanding this factor about how men and women communicate will help us to communicate in a much calmer, healthier way.

I want to share with you the best piece of advice I have ever received when it came to being in a relationship. It was on my wedding day. I was standing in the waiting area with my mother, dressed in my beautiful wedding gown. Everyone else had gone down to get in position. I asked her, "Well mom, any last words of advice or wisdom?" My mom at this time had been happily married to my stepfather for twenty one years, so, she had to know something about making it work, right? She smiled a huge smile and said, "Well honey, when they start driving you crazy, and they will believe me. I want you to go look in the mirror and realize that there is probably a thousand things that you do that drives them crazy, but they never say a word about it because they love you. You are not perfect, so don't start acting like you are. Just love the whole person's faults and all and you will be fine." I have lived this brilliant piece of advice for twenty years and I can honestly say it is true. I am madly in love with my husband, faults and all, and thank God he tolerates mine. We have our little disagreements, don't get me wrong, but I always remember I'm not perfect and that normally does the trick. By the way, my mother and stepfather just celebrated their 41st anniversary and are still going strong.

Control and Communication

"Control" is something everyone strives to have in their life. We all try to maintain a healthy balance between work and home and all of the relationships within the two places. We think that if we can keep control over everything in our life then things will just fall into place and life will be perfect. It would be wonderful if this were true, but the reality is that, we would never learn anything if life were so perfect. After all, I believe that the whole reason we come to earth for a human experience is to learn how to be better human beings and to help each other. If life were perfect what would be the point of leaving heaven in the first place. Having control over life is a complete illusion. The sooner you can accept this, the easier life actually becomes. Begin to learn to roll with whatever life hands you, instead of trying to fight everything all of the time. Resisting life's lesson just prolongs it and that just makes life exhausting and the effort really doesn't change the situation. However, having a good attitude and a sense of humor is crucial and can make or break a situation. Life is constantly evolving. Who you are right now in this moment is not who you were a year ago and who you are now is not who you will be a year from now.

Life experiences change us and if we are lucky, help us to grow. Think of it in broader terms. I want you to remember when you were five years old. What was your view of the world? What did you enjoy doing? What did your clothes and hair look like? Now jump forward five years to ten years old. Did you still see the world the same way? Play with the same toys? I seriously doubt it. You probably considered those things to be "Baby" things. Now jump forward again in your mind to fifteen years old, then twenty, then twenty-five and so on. Can you see how you have changed? Not only do you grow physically, but your views change as you age. This process continues so we have to change with the world and adapt. I would like to think part of this process becomes one of self-acceptance as we get older. For some it's easier than others.

I want to explain what I mean about controlling one's life. I am not referring to decisions like what clothes you wear or what profession you decide to pursue. Nor am I referring to the day to day things like making appointments, grocery shopping, cleaning house, etc. Those are decisions we have to make in order to live productive lives. Those are conscious decisions.

What I am referring to is when life throws you a curve ball just when you thought you had everything going along nicely. You had all the balls in the air in perfect alignment juggling all life has given you. Just then, WHAMMO! Life throws a pillow at your face. That makes it kind of difficult to keep your balance. For instance, you might have a great job and suddenly get fired or maybe have a flat tire in the middle of a rain storm or suddenly be diagnosed with a medical condition. These are things that can be a minor annoyance or all the way up to a devastating situation. You may not have control over what may come your way, but you do at all times have control over how you choose to deal with it. Ten per cent. is the situations, but ninety per cent. is how you proceed when unexpected circumstance comes your way.

Let me give you an example. Recently, my husband and I had just started to get a little bit financially comfortable, when little things began to happen. First, the transmission went out on his car, then the toilet in our main bath began to leak, then literally as he is taking the toilet apart to see what the problem was, the washing machine starts making a noise and suddenly there was a metal rattling and it just stopped. We just looked at each other with an expression of, "Are you kidding me?" All of this happened within the space of a week. Now, it was our choice as to how we were going to react to the events. We could decided to curse the car and appliances and stomp our feet in protest. Then complain to everyone about the situation and how unfair life was to us. The alternative was to face the facts and just deal with the issues as best we could. It wasn't easy at first but, we decided to take the situation with attitude of acceptance of the facts. We didn't like what was happening, but we also couldn't change any of it. So, we took one thing at a time and changed the problem to a positive solution. For instance, we were grateful that we had the savings to fix his car. We didn't want to spend our savings on a transmission but it was still cheaper than a new car and we didn't go into debt. Then we decided to be grateful that he had the knowledge and ability to fix the washing machine and toilet. If we had to call a repairman it could have been very expensive.

Finally, after everything had been fixed again, we decided to become grateful for the physical ability to do the repairs. Human beings rarely really appreciate their magnificent healthy bodies until they decide to quit working. I hope this example gives you some ideas of how to change your behavior when something bad happens. It's always your choice so make a good one.

I know that some people think it makes them feel better to stomp around throwing a hissy fit in front of the world. They say it's getting it out of their systems. However, I completely disagree. What actually happens physiologically to your body and mind can be the equivalent to an all out assault on your physical self. When you let yourself get upset at the situation, your blood pressure rises and your heart rate speeds up. Then, while all of the bodies energy is now distracted by dealing with your outburst, inside, your immune system is lowered and you brain is releasing stress chemicals instead of healthy ones. So, I ask you again to consider what purpose you are actually serving by wasting time throwing your little temper tantrum? It has served zero purpose in resolving the situation and now you have wasted valuable time and energy, which could have been put into fixing the issue or problem. Also, may I point out that you probably feel physically terrible.

The next time something unexpected comes along, try just for a second to step back like a spectator and look at the problem. Some situations can be much more difficult than others, but if you start small it does get easier and your life will begin to get calmer. You will learn to take one issue at a time, deal with it, then move to the next. Try to be in the moment throughout your day. This will help you from getting overwhelmed. I suggest starting with little things like if you get the wrong order at a restaurant, or maybe you accidentally spill something on your favorite shirt. Take a minute and decide how to resolve the issue rather than having a meltdown. It is what it is and it's your choice how to deal with it. This can take a long time to really get good at it, but life is never short of opportunities to practice. Having a calm and peaceful life is worth the work, I promise.

The second kind of control I want to discuss is how we choose to communicate verbally with the people in our lives. It's not just what you say, but it's how you say it. This goes hand in hand with controlling your reactions as previously discussed. Everyone of our loved ones and co-workers could benefit if we could just learn to effectively communicate. Human beings need to learn how tell each other what they want or need and listen to the responses without getting angry or defensive. We must learn to choose our words carefully to be effective. The other thing that is critical is your tone of voice. The same words can have a very different meaning if you use the wrong intonation. Think of this example. Imagine you come in from a date and your best friend is there waiting for you. She is dying to know all of the details. She is so happy for you and asks "So??? How was the date? Did you have a good time? Where did he take you??" Her voice is upbeat and enthusiastic. Of course you would love to tell her everything. Right? Now, let's change it up a bit. Imagine this same scenario of coming home from a date but instead of a friend it's your mother. She is constantly critical and suspicious of your every move. She is always accusing you of making bad choices. Now read through the questions again and imagine the snide, accusing tone being used. I wouldn't want to tell her anything, would you? I'm not saying your mother is like that; it's just an example. I used this example to help you to understand that you must be careful how you get your point across. Another thing I truly detest about communication is the lack of communication. When we withhold all communication and give someone the "Silent Treatment" it's ridiculous. Quit acting like a two-year old pouting. How on earth are you ever going to resolve a problem if you refuse to discuss it?? There are so many traps we can fall into when we arc learning to communicate.

For instance, I have men complain to me all of the time that when they try to find out why a woman is upset they get back, "Well, if you don't know why I'm upset, I'm certainly not going to tell you!" Okay really Princess?? Get off your high horse! I want the men to say back to them, "Great! No problem, I'm going back to what I was doing and you can go off and eat worms. When you're ready to talk about the problem that is bothering you, then let me know." Of course this would go over like a lead balloon, but I think it's funny and the man would feel better. Ha ha.

Seriously, ladies, if your way of controlling a situation is by lack of communication, you have no one to blame but yourself. People, especially men are not mind readers. Women can be very intuitive, but we still aren't mind readers either. We have to verbalize our feelings effectively.

I think the problem begins in our childhood. When I was growing up, I was taught to "Always be polite." Which in "Woman's' World" meant take whatever happens that you don't like, stuff it down inside. You're not allowed to say "No". You're not supposed to hurt anyone else's feelings and you certainly couldn't complain about it. We were supposed to just deal with it. We weren't taught how to express our feelings and emotions, so when we do we try as adults we fail miserably. So many studies have been done showing what happens when feelings aren't expressed and it's all bad news.

Scientists have discovered when this kind of suppression of emotions happens to a woman over a period of time, many things can manifest. There are two ways that negative emotions are dealt with, internally or externally. When we keep hurt feelings and emotions shut down and pushed internally, it will normally manifests in some kind of illness. It may be minor fatigue, colds or the flu. However, it can be as serious as cancer. It is much healthier to express our feelings and emotions externally, but most of us don't know how and it can be devastating to the ones around us. In order to avoid some of the pitfalls in communicating, we have to be aware of the behavior. It is important for both internal and external expression. This behavior changes from childhood to adulthood, but is still the same bad behavior. See if you recognize yourself in some of the more classic examples.

One very popular technique from childhood is, "I'll hold my breath till I turn blue, then you will have to give what I want!!" Okay, if this worked for you then, shame on your parents for succumbing to emotional blackmail. The adult version of this is the famous women's pout. We will sulk around and sigh heavily until you ask the fatal question, "What's wrong honey?" Oh that poor man. This is normally where we give them, "Well, if you don't know I'm not going to tell you." Do I really need to go over that again? I didn't think so. Here is another oldie but goody. The childhood version is, "I'll lie on the floor kicking and screaming until I get my way." In the adult world, this would be ridiculous, so we just kick and scream in our minds. The real reaction is the screaming banshees we have all witnessed at sometime in our lives. They really believe if they yell long enough and loud enough it will work and It might for the short term. However, the consequences long term can be devastating to relationships and health.

I find it fascinating that we are taught so many things growing up about how to behave in public and in groups, but we are never taught how to communicate and express ourselves effectively in a more personal one-on-one situation. Many women either choke down all emotion like "Brie Vandecamp" on "Desperate Housewives". Acting like everything is always fine, and are so caught up in the illusion of image. Some others will become gossipy, snippy women that love to pick apart others to make them feel better. You know the ones I'm talking about. Believe it or not I feel sorry for both of these types of women because they are both in emotional pain and have no way of releasing because they don't know any other way to behave. I believe we aren't taught how to effectively communicate and express our feelings because our parents didn't know how. They couldn't teach us because they weren't taught by their parents and so on. It wasn't until recently in our culture did it become okay to discuss feelings. We were raised to "not air your dirty laundry" and women especially weren't supposed to talk about such things as emotions or feelings or, God forbid, anything fun like the biggie "SEX"!!! We are told to just sit there in your pretty dress and pearls and look cute. Feelings and emotions were considered too personal so they suffered in silence thinking they were the only ones that felt this way.

In some ways many things have evolved over the past fifty years. We have definitely gotten better at acknowledging that we have feelings and emotions and that we are more than robotic Stepford Wives. We can finally own property instead of being property. That's pretty amazing; however, I think we are still in great need of learning how to say what we mean and mean what we say. Believe me, I am not the greatest at this either, but I have found a couple of tips that have proven to work well in the past. First, never try to get your point across when you are yelling so loud that the other person hair is blowing backwards like they are in a wind tunnel. Trust me they are not hearing a word you say. She who talks the loudest doesn't win. Seriously though, always approach a problem after it is not the major issue anymore. Give you both some distance from the intense emotions that you were feeling. Calmer heads lead to calmer solutions. When you are both rational, start the conversation with something like: "I would really like to tell you why I got so upset before, if that's ok." Then in a calm and rational voice explain to them that when they said or did this. . . . it made me feel like this. . . . Let me explain further. For instance, when you didn't call me to let me know you were going to be late, it hurt my feelings, and I didn't know if something had happened to you. When you don't call, I felt like I'm not a priority in your life. I need to feel important in your life and when you take the time out to call I know you are thinking about me and considering how I feel.

A little wordy I know but it makes them understand how you feel without making them defend their position. Which only causes opposition and you will be in an argument all over again. Second, set ground rules for yourself and stick to them. Only you have control over what you will and will not put up with from others. Stop thinking you are not worth being treated like the amazing person that you know you are. Ask yourself, "If I am willing to treat them with dignity and respect then shouldn't I be treated the same way?" Don't you deserve at least that? Of course you do and it's up to you to start taking care of yourself first so that you have enough self-worth to then pass on to others in need. Throughout this book, I have told you over and over how important it is to value yourself first because if you don't, no one else will, and only then can you help other women. This attitude of self loathing will exude from every pore of your body. You will scream to everyone, "DOORMAT! Right here no waiting!!" I know finding your self-worth can be a challenge, but if so many of us "Goddesses with issues" have done it, I know you can too. We are just waiting for you to join us. I support you and believe in you 100 per cent. That is the whole reason I started this project. I want us to band together and start helping each other instead of ripping each other apart. I want all us of to turn our nurturing skills to ourselves first and then find one other woman you see in need and reach out to her. Listen to her and share what you have learned just like I am sharing with you. It might just be a hug or a smile or she may need a good glass of wine and an ear to bend. Try your best to just pass it on. In conclusion pay attention to how you choose to react in the world. What energy you put out comes back to you. I guarantee it. Go in peace as much as you can. Just like the saying goes, "God, grant me the SERENITY to accept the things I cannot change; the COURAGE to change the things I can; and the WISDOM to know the difference." Now go have an amazing life.

The Power of Thought

I believe that in order to change a behavior or belief, first you have to acknowledge the behavior or belief and then question if it is true. We all have these awful, annoying, hurtful voices in our heads that tell us incessantly about all of our faults and shortcomings. Why we are not worthy to receive all the world has to offer. That is a lie! Fortunately, I believe we also have encouraging voices that tell us we can achieve our dreams! I recently heard the most wonderful saying that I think is a good place to begin. Author Abraham-Hicks states, "A belief is only a thought that you keep thinking". Whatever you believe about yourself is absolutely right because you believe it. You create your reality through your thoughts. In other words, if you don't believe you are worthy of abundance, of everything life has to offer, then you won't ever achieve it. Your thoughts will self-sabotage anything that comes your way that is good and you will not receive it. So where do you start to break down your beliefs? Every thought you think has an energy or vibration that causes you to feel a certain way. Simply put bad thoughts make you feel bad and good thoughts make you feel good. It really is that simple. You must learn to control your "Monkey Mind" or it will control you. With time and practice you will learn to control your own patterns of thought and you will be able to change directions in an instant.

Let me give you an example. I want you to think back to a time when you had a bad day. Let's say, it started when you woke up late for work which put you in a panic. Then, you couldn't find anything to wear (that you liked). You proceed to the kitchen and burn your tongue on hot coffee, Trip going out the door and the traffic is awful so you're late and the boss is angry. I get anxious just thinking about it. I'm sure it seemed like your day was spiraling out of control and it just kept getting worse and you felt helpless to control it. Well, guess what? The reason it spiraled out of control was because your energy was focused on the negative aspects, starting with waking up late.

The negative energy you felt went directly from your brain to all parts of your physical body and out to the universe. Your energy is like a magnet. "Like attracts like" You were emitting a signal to continue bringing more negative things because energy was focused on the negative situation. Remember in the earlier chapters I talked about, it's always your choice in how you react to a situation. It applies to every aspect of your life. I know this may sound crazy, but it really is the truth. The sooner you can get a grip on your emotions, the calmer your life will become. I guarantee it. Now let's use the same scenario, but a much different outcome.

Picture yourself waking up feeling refreshed after a great night's sleep. There is plenty of time to prepare your day. You sail through getting ready for work; your clothes make you feel like a million bucks. You smile to yourself thinking what a beautiful day it's going to be. The chemicals and energies your brain releases sends out an almost, "Can't touch me" signal. Everything seems to go your way. I know you have experienced both occurrences in your life so the issue is how you choose to think!

There are several areas of our lives that affect our thoughts and how we interact in the world. The best way to figure out which is working and which needs work is break it up into sections. Take a good look at each part and see where you might want to redefine yourself and where you really want to be in your life. Remember, a belief is only a thought you keep thinking, so change your thoughts, change your energy and your life. Through my education I have learned that there are six main areas in a person's life that need to be balanced. If one of the areas is out of balance, then the whole structure is on shaky ground. These areas are: Professional, Financial, Wellness, Relationships, Emotional, and Spiritual.

I want you to do the following—on six separate sheets of paper, write on the top of each one a different area, like "Professional, Emotional" etc. Next, I want you to write a number from one to ten on how you would rate yourself in that area. Take the time to describe why you gave yourself that score and in detail how you think you can improve it. You have to be brutally honest with yourself or this is futile and you won't change. In some areas, you may give yourself a very high score so those would be the last areas to be concerned with for now. Next, take a look at the ones that your score was less than desirable. Choose one that you would like to work on first. Only work on one area at a time because change is a marathon not a sprint. You should be patient with yourself. New habits take time to become ingrained. I like my clients to make a declaration of what action they are going to take and make a specific timeline for achieving it. There can't be progress unless you hold yourself accountable. If for whatever reason you don't achieve your goal, ask yourself why and again be honest. Don't get caught in a blame game. Only you are responsible for your actions and your life. Own up to it. Don't beat yourself up. That is a complete waste of time and spirit. You are a magnificent work in progress. If you are learning then, you are growing and may we all be ten feet tall when we die. Figuratively of course, not literally.

This process will take time. This is one of the best techniques I have ever learned when it comes to changing your behavior. Being a life coach is wonderful, but the real work always has to come from the client. I have counseled many women that are focused on the outside instead of the inside. Some will spend their whole lives in search of the illusive fix. Guess what? You are your own fix. Not the guy at the end of the bar, or at the checkout stand or at the office. I guarantee you that the more you focus on fixing the real you, the more attractive and confident you will be to others. If you really want a man, then know that the last thing he wants is a needy chick hanging on to him. You have to know who you are and what you want in life. Be a partner not a leach. That's how this whole book got started in the first place. However, it quickly changed into a much more serious endeavor. It became my goal to really help change women's views and behavior. It is my passion to get women to wake up, and take control of their lives. Your life is happening now, not when Mr. Wonderful comes along. Don't let it pass you by without enjoying it. Live in the moment and live in gratitude. Start every morning with a statement of gratitude and it will set the tone for your day. Things will begin to fall into place.

So, ladies, in conclusion, I hope this book has helped you in some way because that is its sole intent. At the very least I hope it gave you some things to think about and be grateful for in your life. I truly wish all of you the abundance life has to offer. I look forward to hearing your stories in the future. Always care more for your wellbeing and you will be a blessing to others! Be your own best friend and learn to love the one and only you. Remember—"She Who Care the Least Wins!" Don't be desperate, be fabulous! Womankind Rocks!

The Plan

S o, now it's all up to you. From now on everything you do is your choice. No excuses. From the time you wake up in the morning everything becomes your choice. Will you decide to be in a good mood or bad? Will you be kind to your loved ones or snap their heads off for no reason? Even when your entire day seems to be going badly, it is still your choice to stop! Examine how you're reacting to what's happening, then change direction if you need to. The energy you give off will directly affect the energy around you and bring the equivalent.

I hope after reading this manifesto of mine you will have some ideas about how you became who you are and what has influenced you thus far. We all start off having to do what our parents and teachers tell us. However, at some point in your life, you have to decide to become your own master. Good decisions or bad you must own up to it and take the chance. Put it all on the line and see what happens. Take the road less traveled if you feel compelled too. I realize that, in the beginning, stepping out can be scary; but ask one simple question: "If I don't do this (fill in the blank) will I regret it when I'm eighty? Because, of course, by then you will probably be too old to do whatever it is anyway. This question has made me be more adventurous and I have not regretted the decisions I made. I have found that regret serves no purpose but to annoy the hell out me, so I don't look back anymore. It's a complete waste of spirit. I can't change the past but I can affect the future.

In my life so far I have achieved six different degrees, all in different areas. I have enjoyed getting to try many different lines of work and met some amazing people along the way. My life has been an amazing adventure. The best part is that I'm not done yet. I have lived overseas and even learned how to ride a motorcycle. I love trying new things. My first forty years I had to get my education and get my life in order. Now, the next forty years are whatever I choose them to be. I truly feel like I'm just getting started. Even when it comes to writing this book, it was something that I felt compelled to do. I don't even know whether anyone will ever read this but it really doesn't matter because I wanted to do it. So I did. So, that's all there is. The end! Ha Ha. So, maybe you should begin your journey with, what am I compelled to do? Where do I want to go next? What is my passion? When I am fortunate enough to get this published I have one deep hope and desire. That this little manifesto that I have written will get women talking and thinking about the choices they make in their lives. If this actually helps to get them motivated to change something that they don't like or help to avoid some of our mistakes, then AMEN!! That would just be icing on the cake.

So, my plan is to continue every day to learn more about myself and the world around me. To be kind to others because they are also on their journey and are doing the best they know, just like me. If they offend you, forgive them and move on. You may not agree with them, but you should respect them just the same. Finally, I pray that my existence has made some contribution to the world rather than taking from it. I believe that is why we are all here on this planet. We have all been blessed with God-given talents that we need to use to be of service to others.

So, what is your God given gift? How are you going to find it? So what's your plan going to be? It's up to you. Well, I guess that's it. I'm now going to turn this book over to God and the Universe and see what happens and where my life will lead me next. This will be fun!! I love a great adventure! I'll keep you posted!!!

CPSIA information can be obtained at www.ICGtesting.com
Printed in the USA
BVOW05s2157010414

349484BV00001B/8/P